QUICK CROCHET

Home Décor

LEISURE ARTS, INC.
Maumelle, Arkansas

Choose from quick and easy projects to enhance your home. Most everyone can use a basket for stashing yarn or a cuddly afghan for a lazy day. Deck your halls with a colorful, stash-busting garland and toss a colorful rug onto your floor. With pillows, frames, and flowerpot cozies, it will be hard to pick which one to crochet first! Most are worked with super bulky weight yarns which allows for fast and gorgeous results.

CONTENTS

ALABASTER AFGHAN

●●○○ EASY

Finished Size: 50" x 63½" (127 cm x 161.5 cm)

shopping list

Yarn (Super Bulky Weight)

[6 ounces, 106 yards (170 grams, 97 meters) per skein]:

○ 13 skeins

Crochet Hook

○ Size P (11.5 mm) **or** size needed for gauge

gauge information

In Center pattern,

8 sts (hdc and chs) and 5 rows = 4" (10 cm)

Gauge Swatch: 6½" wide x 4" high (16.5 cm x 10 cm)

Ch 14.

Row 1: Hdc in fourth ch from hook **(3 skipped chs count as first hdc plus ch 1)**, ★ ch 1, skip next ch, hdc in next ch; repeat from ★ across: 7 hdc and 6 ch-1 sps.

Row 2: Ch 2 **(counts as first hdc)**, turn; hdc in next ch-1 sp, ★ ch 1, hdc in next ch-1 sp; repeat from ★ across to last hdc, hdc in last hdc: 8 hdc and 5 ch-1 sps.

Row 3: Ch 3 **(counts as first hdc plus ch 1)**, turn; ★ skip next hdc, hdc in next ch-1 sp, ch 1; repeat from ★ across to last 2 hdc, skip next hdc, hdc in last hdc: 7 hdc and 6 ch-1 sps.

Rows 4 and 5: Repeat Rows 2 and 3: 7 hdc and 6 ch-1 sps. Finish off.

stitch guide

PUFF ST (uses one dc)

★ YO, insert hook from **front** to **back** around post of dc just made *(Fig. 3, page 43)*, YO and pull up a loop; repeat from ★ once **more**, YO and draw through all 5 loops on hook.

DOUBLE CROCHET 2 TOGETHER *(abbreviated dc2tog)* (uses one hdc and one ch-1 sp)

★ YO, insert hook in **next** st or sp, YO and pull up a loop, YO and draw through 2 loops on hook; repeat from ★ once **more**, YO and draw through all 3 loops on hook **(counts as one dc)**.

bottom border

Ch 102.

Row 1 (Right side)**:** Working in back ridge of beginning ch *(Fig. 1, page 43)*, dc in fourth ch from hook **(3 skipped chs count as first dc)** and in each ch across: 100 dc.

Note: Loop a short piece of yarn around any stitch to mark Row 1 as **right** side.

Row 2: Ch 3 **(counts as first dc)**, turn; dc in next dc, ★ work Puff St, skip next dc, dc in next dc; repeat from ★ across: 67 dc and 33 Puff Sts.

Row 3: Ch 3 **(counts as first dc)**, turn; dc in next st and in each st across: 100 dc.

Rows 4 and 5: Repeat Rows 2 and 3; do **not** finish off: 100 dc.

center

Row 1: Ch 3 **(counts as first hdc plus ch 1)**, turn; hdc in next dc, ch 1, skip next dc, hdc in next dc, ch 1, skip next dc, ★ † (hdc in next dc, ch 1) 3 times, skip next dc, hdc in next dc, ch 1, skip next dc, (hdc in next dc, ch 1) twice, skip next dc †, hdc in next dc, ch 1, skip next dc; repeat from ★ once **more**, **[**(hdc in next dc, ch 1) twice, skip next dc, hdc in next dc, ch 1, skip next dc**]** twice, (hdc in next dc, ch 1) 4 times, **[**skip next dc, hdc in next dc, ch 1, skip next dc, (hdc in next dc, ch 1) twice**]** 2 times, skip next dc, repeat from † to † twice, (hdc in next dc, ch 1, skip next dc, repeat from † to † once) 2 times, hdc in next dc, ch 1, skip next dc, (hdc in next dc, ch 1) twice, skip next dc, hdc in next dc, ch 1, skip next dc, hdc in last dc: 64 hdc and 63 ch-1 sps.

Row 2: Ch 2 **(counts as first hdc)**, turn; hdc in next ch-1 sp, (ch 1, hdc in next ch-1 sp) across to last hdc, hdc in last hdc: 65 hdc and 62 ch-1 sps.

Row 3: Ch 3 **(counts as first hdc plus ch 1)**, turn; ★ skip next hdc, hdc in next ch-1 sp, ch 1; repeat from ★ across to last 2 hdc, skip next hdc, hdc in last hdc: 64 hdc and 63 ch-1 sps.

Repeat Rows 2 and 3 for pattern until piece measures aproximately 44" (112 cm) from beginning ch, ending by working Row 3; do **not** finish off.

top border

Row 1: Ch 3 **(counts as first dc)**, turn; dc in next 3 sts, ★ dc2tog, dc in next 2 sts, dc2tog, dc in next 3 sts, dc2tog; repeat from ★ 8 times **more**, dc in last 24 sts: 100 dc.

Rows 2-5: Work same as Rows 2-5 of Bottom Border; at end of Row 5, finish off.

Make 4, 9" (23 cm) long tassels ***(Figs. 5a & b, page 45)***. Attach one tassel to each corner of Afghan.

STILL FOG BASKET

●●○○ **EASY**

Finished Size: 10" diameter x 8½" high (25.5 cm x 21.5 cm)

shopping list

Yarn (Bulky Weight)

[8.8 ounces, 317 yards (250 grams, 290 meters) per skein]:

- ○ Taupe - 2 skeins
- ○ Cream - 1 skein

Crochet Hook

- ○ Size L (8 mm) **or** size needed for gauge

gauge information

With two strands of yarn held together,
9 sc and 9 rnds = 4" (10 cm)

Gauge Swatch: 4" (10 cm) diameter

Work same as Basket on page 10 through Rnd 4: 24 sc.

basket

Holding 2 strands of Taupe together, ch 4; join with slip st to form a ring.

Rnd 1 (Right side)**:** Ch 1, 6 sc in ring; do **not** join; place marker to indicate beginning of rnd ***(see Markers, page 42)***.

Note: Loop a short piece of yarn around any stitch to mark Rnd 1 as **right** side.

Rnd 2: 2 Sc in each sc around: 12 sc.

Rnd 3: (Sc in next sc, 2 sc in next sc) around: 18 sc.

Rnd 4: (2 Sc in next sc, sc in next 2 sc) around: 24 sc.

Rnd 5: Sc in next sc, 2 sc in next sc, (sc in next 3 sc, 2 sc in next sc) around to last 2 sc, sc in last 2 sc: 30 sc.

Rnd 6: Sc in next 3 sc, 2 sc in next sc, (sc in next 4 sc, 2 sc in next sc) around to last sc, sc in last sc: 36 sc.

Rnd 7: (2 Sc in next sc, sc in next 5 sc) around: 42 sc.

Rnd 8: Sc in next 2 sc, 2 sc in next sc, (sc in next 6 sc, 2 sc in next sc) around to last 4 sc, sc in last 4 sc: 48 sc.

Rnd 9: Sc in next 5 sc, 2 sc in next sc, (sc in next 7 sc, 2 sc in next sc) around to last 2 sc, sc in last 2 sc: 54 sc.

Rnd 10: (2 Sc in next sc, sc in next 8 sc) around: 60 sc.

Rnd 11: Sc in next 2 sc, 2 sc in next sc, (sc in next 9 sc, 2 sc in next sc) around to last 7 sc, sc in last 7 sc: 66 sc.

Rnd 12: Sc in Back Loop Only of each sc around ***(Fig. 2, page 43)***.

Rnds 13-24: Sc in both loops of each sc around.

Rnd 25: Sc in each sc around, changing to two strands of Cream in last sc *(Fig. 4b, page 44)*, cut Taupe.

Rnds 26-28: Sc in each sc around.

Rnd 29: Sc in next 13 sc, ch 8, skip next 8 sc, sc in next 25 sc, ch 8, skip next 8 sc, sc in next 12 sc: 50 sc and 16 chs.

Rnd 30: Sc in next 13 sc, sc in back ridge of next 8 chs ***(Fig. 1, page 43)***, sc in next 25 sc, sc in back ridge of next 8 chs, sc in next 12 sc: 66 sc.

Rnd 31: Sc in each sc around.

Slip st in next sc; finish off.

FAWNBAY FLOOR PILLOW

EASY

Finished Size: 24" (61 cm) square

shopping list

Yarn (Super Bulky Weight)
[5 ounces, 87 yards (140 grams, 80 meters) per skein]:
- ○ Brown - 6 skeins

[6 ounces, 106 yards (170 grams, 97 meters) per skein]:
- ○ Dk Brown - 1 skein
- ○ Cream - 1 skein

Crochet Hook
- ○ Size L (8 mm) **or** size needed for gauge

Additional Supplies
- ○ 24" (61 cm) square pillow form

gauge information

In pattern, 13 sts (sc and chs) = 6½" (16.5 cm);
12 rows = 5¾" (14.5 cm)

Gauge Swatch: 6½" wide x 5¾" high (16.5 cm x 14.5 cm)

Ch 14.

Row 1: Sc in second ch from hook, ★ ch 1, skip next ch, sc in next ch; repeat from ★ across: 7 sc and 6 ch-1 sps.

Row 2: Ch 1, turn; sc in first sc and in next ch-1 sp, (ch 1, sc in next ch-1 sp) across to last sc, sc in last sc: 8 sc and 5 ch-1 sps.

Row 3: Ch 1, turn sc in first sc, ch 1, (sc in next ch-1 sp, ch 1) across to last 2 sc, skip next sc, sc in last sc: 7 sc and 6 ch-1 sps.

Rows 4-12: Repeat Rows 2 and 3, 4 times; then repeat Row 2 once **more**.

Finish off.

back

With Brown, ch 48.

Row 1 (Right side)**:** Sc in second ch from hook, ★ ch 1, skip next ch, sc in next ch; repeat from ★ across: 24 sc and 23 ch-1 sps.

Note: Loop a short piece of yarn around any stitch to mark Row 1 as **right** side.

Row 2: Ch 1, turn; sc in first sc and in next ch-1 sp, (ch 1, sc in next ch-1 sp) across to last sc, sc in last sc: 25 sc and 22 ch-1 sps.

Row 3: Ch 1, turn; sc in first sc, ch 1, (sc in next ch-1 sp, ch 1) across to last 2 sc, skip next sc, sc in last sc: 24 sc and 23 ch-1 sps.

Rows 4-51: Repeat Rows 2 and 3, 24 times: 24 sc and 23 ch-1 sps.

Finish off.

front

Work same as Back through Row 20, changing to Dk Brown in last sc *(Fig. 4a, page 44)*, drop Brown: 25 sc and 22 ch-1 sps.

Row 21: Ch 1, turn; sc in first sc, ch 1, (sc in next ch-1 sp, ch 1) across to last 2 sc, skip next sc, sc in last sc changing to Cream, drop Dk Brown: 24 sc and 23 ch-1 sps.

Row 22: Ch 1, turn; sc in first sc and in next ch-1 sp, (ch 1, sc in next ch-1 sp) across to last sc, sc in last sc changing to Brown, drop Cream: 25 sc and 22 ch-1 sps.

Row 23: Ch 1, turn; sc in first sc, ch 1, (sc in next ch-1 sp, ch 1) across to last 2 sc, skip next sc, sc in last sc changing to Dk Brown, drop Brown: 24 sc and 23 ch-1 sps.

Rows 24-28: Repeat Rows 21-23 once, then repeat Rows 21 and 22 once **more.**: 25 sc and 22 ch-1 sps.

Cut Dk Brown and Cream.

Row 29: Repeat Row 3 of Back: 24 sc and 23 ch-1 sps.

Rows 30-51: With Brown, repeat Rows 2 and 3 of Back, 11 times; at end of Row 51, do **not** finish off.

joining

With **wrong** sides of Row 51 together, with Front facing, and working through **both** layers, sc evenly around working 2 sc in each corner and inserting pillow form before closing; join with slip st to first sc, finish off.

GO-GO GARLAND

EASY

Finished Size: Approximately 3 yards (2.75 meters) long

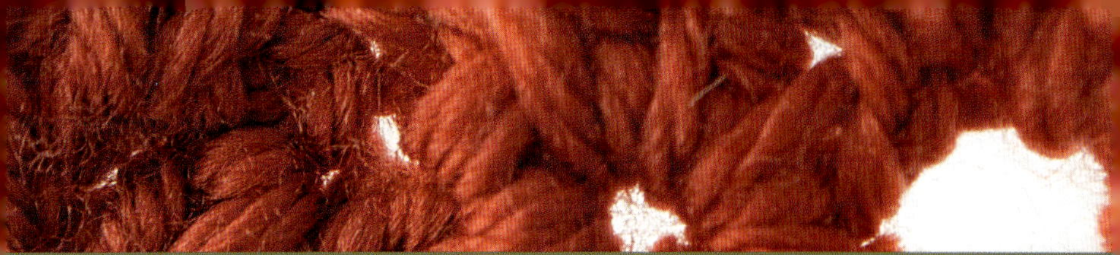

It takes just a few yards of each color to make this colorful garland. It's a great way to use up partial balls, and it's easy to make the garland as long as you like.

shopping list

Yarn (Medium Weight) MEDIUM 4

[5 ounces, 256 yards (141 grams, 234 meters) per skein**]**:

- ○ Green - 25 yards (23 meters)
- ○ Dk Orange - 25 yards (23 meters)
- ○ Purple - 25 yards (23 meters)
- ○ Teal - 25 yards (23 meters)
- ○ Lt Orange - 25 yards (23 meters)
- ○ Lt Gold - 15 yards (13.5 meters)

Crochet Hook

- ○ Size H (5 mm)

gauge information

Gauge is not of great importance; your Garland may be a little larger or smaller without changing the overall effect.

triangle

(Make 5 **each** with Green, Dk Orange, Purple, Teal, and Lt Orange)

Ch 4; join with slip st to form a ring.

Rnd 1 (Right side)**:** Ch 3 **(counts as first dc, now and throughout)**, 2 dc in ring, ch 3, (3 dc in ring, ch 3) twice; join with slip st to first dc: 9 dc and 3 ch-3 sps.

Note: Loop a short piece of yarn around any stitch to mark Rnd 1 as **right** side.

Rnd 2: Ch 3, dc in next 2 dc, (3 dc, ch 3, 3 dc) in next ch-3 sp, ★ dc in next 3 dc, (3 dc, ch 3, 3 dc) in next ch-3 sp; repeat from ★ once **more**; join with slip st to first dc, finish off.

joining

Join Triangles in the following order: ★ Green, Dk Orange, Purple, Teal, Lt Orange; repeat from ★ across.

Triangle Joining: With Lt Gold, ch 52; with **right** side of each Triangle facing and holding yarn to **wrong** side, slip st in next 9 dc across one edge of first Triangle, ★ ch 4, slip st in next 9 dc of next Triangle; repeat from ★ until all Triangles are joined, ch 52; finish off.

THROW RUG

EASY

Finished Size: 24" (61 cm) diameter

shopping list

Yarn (Super Bulky Weight)

[8 ounces, 149 yards (227 grams, 136 meters) per skein]:

- ○ Taupe - 2 skeins
- ○ Navy - 1 skein
- ○ Pink - 1 skein

Crochet Hook

- ○ Size M/N (9 mm) **or** size needed for gauge

gauge information

Gauge Swatch: 4" (10 cm) diameter

Work same as Rug on page 22 through Rnd 2: 24 dc.

rug

With Navy, ch 5; join with slip st to form a ring.

Rnd 1 (Right side)**:** Ch 4 **(counts as first dc plus ch 1)**, (dc in ring, ch 1) 5 times; join with slip st to first dc, finish off: 6 dc and 6 ch-1 sps.

Note: Loop a short piece of yarn around any stitch to mark Rnd 1 as **right** side.

Rnd 2: With **right** side facing, join Taupe with dc in any dc ***(see Joining With Dc, page 42)***; dc in same st, 2 dc in next ch-1 sp and in each dc and each ch-1 sp around; join with slip st to first dc, finish off: 24 dc.

Rnd 3: With **right** side facing, join Pink with dc in any dc; 2 dc in same st, ch 2, skip next 2 dc, ★ 3 dc in next dc, ch 2, skip next 2 dc; repeat from ★ around; join with slip st to first dc, finish off: 24 dc and 8 ch-2 sps.

Rnd 4: With **right** side facing, join Taupe with dc in any ch-2 sp; 2 dc in same sp, dc in next 3 dc, ★ 3 dc in next ch-2 sp, dc in next 3 dc; repeat from ★ around; join with slip st to first dc, finish off: 48 dc.

Rnd 5: With **right** side facing, join Navy with dc in center dc of any 3-dc group; 2 dc in same st, ch 1, skip next 2 dc, ★ 3 dc in next dc, ch 1, skip next 2 dc; repeat from ★ around; join with slip st to first dc, finish off: 48 dc and 16 ch-1 sps.

Rnd 6: With **right** side facing, join Taupe with dc in any ch-1 sp; dc in next 3 dc, 2 dc in next ch-1 sp, dc in next 3 dc, ★ dc in next ch-1 sp and in next 3 dc, 2 dc in next ch-1 sp, dc in next 3 dc; repeat from ★ around; join with slip st to first dc, do **not** finish off: 72 dc.

Rnd 7: Ch 3 (**counts as first dc, now and throughout**), dc in next 3 dc, 2 dc in next dc, ★ dc in next 5 dc, 2 dc in next dc; repeat from ★ around to last dc, dc in last dc; join with slip st to first dc, finish off: 84 dc.

Rnd 8: With **right** side facing, skip first 3 dc and join Navy with dc in next dc; 2 dc in same st, ch 1, skip next 2 dc, 3 dc in next dc, ch 1, (skip next 3 dc, 3 dc in next dc, ch 1) twice, † skip next 2 dc, 3 dc in next dc, ch 1, skip next 3 dc, 3 dc in next dc, ch 1 †; repeat from † to † 6 times **more**, (skip next 2 dc, 3 dc in next dc, ch 1) twice, repeat from † to † twice, skip last 3 dc; join with slip st to first dc, finish off: 72 dc and 24 ch-1 sps.

Rnd 9: With **right** side facing, join Taupe with dc in any ch-1 sp; dc in next 3 dc, 2 dc in next ch-1 sp, dc in next 3 dc, ★ dc in next ch-1 sp and in next 3 dc, 2 dc in next ch-1 sp, dc in next 3 dc; repeat from ★ around; join with slip st to first dc, do **not** finish off: 108 dc.

Rnd 10: Ch 3, dc in next 7 dc, 2 dc in next dc, (dc in next 8 dc, 2 dc in next dc) around; join with slip st to first dc: 120 dc.

Rnd 11: Ch 3, dc in next 3 dc, 2 dc in next dc, (dc in next 9 dc, 2 dc in next dc) around to last 5 dc, dc in last 5 dc; join with slip st to first dc, finish off: 132 dc.

Rnd 12: With **right** side facing, join Pink with dc in any dc; 2 dc in same st, skip next 2 dc, (3 dc in next dc, skip next 2 dc) around; join with slip st to first dc, finish off.

Rnd 13: With **right** side facing, join Taupe with dc in any dc; dc in next 9 dc, 2 dc in next dc, (dc in next 10 dc, 2 dc in next dc) around; join with slip st to first dc, do **not** finish off: 144 dc.

Rnd 14: Ch 1, sc in same st as joining and in each dc around; join with slip st to first sc, finish off.

BLOSSOM FRAMES

●●○○ **EASY**

Small - Approximately 9½" (24 cm) diameter
Large - Approximately 11" (28 cm) diameter

shopping list

Yarn (Medium Weight)
[3.5 ounces, 186 yards (100 grams, 170 meters) per ball]:

- ○ Taupe - 1 ball
- ○ Blue - 1 ball
- ○ Lt Blue - 1 ball
- ○ Ecru - 1 ball

Crochet Hook

- ○ Size G (4 mm)

Additional Supplies

- ○ Yarn needle
- ○ 6" (15 cm) wood embroidery hoop
- ○ 8" (20.5 cm) wood embroidery hoop

gauge information

Gauge is not of great importance, although stitches should be worked fairly firmly.

large frame

Separate inner and outer hoops of large embroidery hoop; set outer hoop aside.

Rnd 1 (Right side)**:** With Taupe, work 200 sc around inner hoop; join with slip st to first sc, finish off.

Note: Loop a short piece of yarn around any stitch to mark Rnd 1 as **right** side.

Rnd 2: With **right** side facing and Ecru, holding slip knot and yarn to **wrong** side, insert hook in first sc, hook loop and pull through st; (skip next sc, slip st in next sc) around to last sc; cut yarn leaving a 6" (15 cm) end, draw end through loop on hook. Thread yarn needle with end; skip last sc, insert needle under both loops of first slip st and pull yarn through; insert needle back through center of last slip st and secure end.

Rnd 3: With **right** side facing and working in sc on Rnd 1, join Blue with sc any sc ***(see Joining With Sc, page 42)***; skip next 3 sc, 5 dc in next sc, skip next 3 sc, ★ sc in next sc, skip next 3 sc, 5 dc in next sc, skip next 3 sc; repeat from ★ around; join with slip st to first sc, finish off: 25 5-dc groups and 25 sc.

Rnd 4: With **right** side facing, join Lt Blue with sc in center dc of any 5-dc group; skip next 2 dc, 7 dc in next sc, skip next 2 dc, ★ sc in next dc, skip next 2 dc, 7 dc in next sc, skip next 2 dc; repeat from ★ around; join with slip st to first sc, finish off: 25 7-dc groups and 25 sc.

Rnd 5: With **right** side facing, join Ecru with sc in center dc of any 7-dc group; skip next 3 dc, 9 dc in next sc, skip next 3 dc, ★ sc in next dc, skip next 3 dc, 9 dc in next sc, skip next 3 dc; repeat from ★ around; join with slip st to first sc, finish off.

small frame

Separate inner and outer hoops of small embroidery hoop; set outer hoop aside.

Rnd 1 (Right side)**:** With Taupe, work 152 sc around inner hoop; join with slip st to first sc, finish off.

Note: Mark Rnd 1 as **right** side.

Rnd 2: With Blue, work same as Rnd 2 of Large Frame.

Rnd 3: With **right** side facing and working in sc on Rnd 1, join Lt Blue with sc in any sc; ★ ch 4, skip next 3 sc, sc in next sc; repeat from ★ around to last 3 sc, ch 1, skip last 3 sc, dc in first sc to form last ch-4 sp: 38 ch-4 sps.

Rnd 4: Ch 3 (**counts as first dc, now and throughout**), 3 dc in last ch-4 sp made, ch 2, sc in next ch-4 sp, ch 2, ★ 4 dc in next ch-4 sp, ch 2, sc in next ch-4 sp, ch 2; repeat from ★ around; join with slip st to first dc, finish off: 19 4-dc groups, 19 sc, and 38 ch-2 sps.

Rnd 5: With **right** side facing, join Blue with sc in last ch-2 sp; ch 4, skip next 4 dc, sc in next ch-2 sp, ★ ch 4, skip next sc, sc in next ch-2 sp, ch 4, skip next 4 dc, sc in next ch-2 sp; repeat from ★ around to last sc, ch 1, skip last sc, dc in first sc to form last ch-4 sp: 38 ch-4 sps.

Rnd 6: Ch 3, 3 dc in last ch-4 sp made, ch 2, sc in next ch-4 sp, ch 2, ★ 4 dc in next ch-4 sp, ch 2, sc in next ch-4 sp, ch 2; repeat from ★ around; join with slip st to first dc, finish off.

both frames

Replace outer hoops and tighten screws. Use screw assemblies as hangers.

TOASTY TASSELS PILLOW

EASY

Finished Size: 18" (45.5 cm) square

shopping list

Yarn (Super Bulky Weight)
[5 ounces, 87 yards (140 grams, 80 meters) per skein]:

- ○ 4 skeins

Crochet Hook

- ○ Size M/N (9 mm) **or** size needed for gauge

Additional Supplies

- ○ 18" (45.5 cm) square pillow form
- ○ Yarn needle
- ○ Pins

gauge information

7 hdc and 6 rows = 4" (10 cm)

Gauge Swatch: 4" (10 cm) square

Ch 8.

Row 1: Hdc in third ch from hook and in each ch across: 7 sts.

Rows 2-6: Ch 2 **(counts as first hdc)**, turn; hdc in next hdc and in each st across.

Finish off.

stitch guide

PUFF STITCH (uses one dc)

★ YO, insert hook from **front** to **back** around post of dc just made ***(Fig. 3, page 43)***, YO and pull up a loop; repeat from ★ once **more**, YO and draw through all 5 loops on hook.

back

Ch 29.

Row 1 (Wrong side)**:** Hdc in third ch from hook and in each ch across **(2 skipped chs count as first hdc, now and throughout)**: 28 hdc.

Note: Loop a short piece of yarn around the **back** of any stitch on Row 1 to mark **right** side.

Rows 2-23: Ch 2 **(counts as first hdc, now and throughout)**, turn; hdc in next hdc and in each hdc across.

Finish off.

front lower half

Ch 29.

Row 1 (Right side)**:** Hdc in third ch from hook and in each ch across: 28 hdc.

Note: Mark Row 1 as **right** side.

Rows 2-13: Ch 2, turn; hdc in next hdc and in each hdc across.

Finish off.

front upper half

Ch 29.

Row 1 (Wrong side)**:** Hdc in third ch from hook and in each ch across: 28 hdc.

Note: Mark the **back** of any stitch on Row 1 as **right** side.

Rows 2-7: Ch 2, turn; hdc in next hdc and in each hdc across.

Row 8: Ch 3 **(counts as first dc, now and throughout)**, turn; ★ dc in next 2 hdc, work Puff St, skip next hdc; repeat from ★ across to last 3 hdc, dc in last 3 hdc: 20 dc and 8 Puff Sts.

Row 9: Ch 2, turn; hdc in next dc and in each dc across: 28 hdc.

Row 10: Ch 3, turn; dc in next hdc, work Puff St, ★ skip next hdc, dc in next 2 hdc, work Puff St; repeat from ★ across to last hdc, dc in last hdc: 19 dc and 9 Puff Sts.

Row 11: Ch 2, turn; hdc in next dc and in each dc across: 28 hdc.

Row 12: Ch 2, turn; hdc in next hdc and in each hdc across; finish off.

finishing

With **wrong** sides together, pin Front Upper and Lower Halves to Back, with Rows 11 and 12 of Upper Half overlapping Rows 1 and 2 of Lower Half.

With Fronts facing and working through **all** layers, join yarn with sc in any corner st *(**see Joining With Sc, page 42**)*; 2 sc in same st, sc evenly around working 3 sc in each corner; join with slip st to first sc, finish off.

Insert pillow form.

Tack Upper Half to Lower Half.

tassel

Make 3, 6" (15 cm) long tassels *(**Figs. 5a & b, page 45**)*. Using photo as as guide for placement, attach Tassels to Row 12 of Upper Half.

FLOWERPOT COZIES

●●○○ **EASY**

Finished Sizes:

Small: fits $3^5/_8$" (9 cm) diameter bottom pot

Medium: fits 4½" (11.5 cm) bottom diameter pot

shopping list

Yarn (Medium Weight) 4 MEDIUM

[5 ounces, 280 yards (140 grams, 256 meters) per skein]:

- ○ 1 skein will make both Cozies

Crochet Hook

- ○ Size H (5 mm) **or** size needed for gauge

gauge information

13 sc and 13 rnds = 4" (10 cm)

Gauge Swatch: 3" (7.5 cm) diameter

Work same as Small Cozy on page 34 through Rnd 5: 30 sc.

small cozy

Ch 4; join with slip st to form a ring.

Rnd 1 (Right side)**:** Ch 1, 6 sc in ring; do **not** join, place marker to indicate beginning of rnd ***(see Markers, page 42)***.

Rnd 2: 2 Sc in each sc around: 12 sc.

Rnd 3: (Sc in next sc, 2 sc in next sc) around: 18 sc.

Rnd 4: (Sc in next 2 sc, 2 sc in next sc) around: 24 sc.

Rnd 5: Sc in next sc, 2 sc in next sc, (sc in next 3 sc, 2 sc in next sc) around to last 2 sc, sc in last 2 sc: 30 sc.

Rnd 6: Sc in next 3 sc, 2 sc in next sc, (sc in next 4 sc, 2 sc in next sc) around to last sc, sc in last sc: 36 sc.

Rnd 7: (Sc in next 5 sc, 2 sc in next sc) around: 42 sc.

Rnds 8-14: Sc in each sc around.

Rnd 15: (Sc in next 13 sc, 2 sc in next sc) around: 45 sc.

Rnds 16 and 17: Sc in each sc around.

Rnd 18: Sc in next 7 sc, 2 sc in next sc, (sc in next 14 sc, 2 sc in next sc) twice, sc in next 7 sc: 48 sc.

Rnd 19: Sc in each sc around.

Rnd 20: (Sc in next 15 sc, 2 sc in next sc) around: 51 sc.

Rnds 21-23: Sc in each sc around.

Rnd 24: ★ Sc in next 4 sc, 2 sc in next sc, sc in next 8 sc, 2 sc in next sc, sc in next 3 sc; repeat from ★ around: 57 sc.

Rnds 25-28: Sc in each sc around.

Rnd 29: Slip st in each sc around; finish off.

medium cozy

Work same as Small Cozy through Rnd 7: 42 sc.

Rnd 8: Sc in next 3 sc, 2 sc in next sc, (sc in next 6 sc, 2 sc in next sc) around to last 3 sc, sc in last 3 sc: 48 sc.

Rnds 9-20: Sc in each sc around.

Rnd 21: (Sc in next 15 sc, 2 sc in next sc) around: 51 sc.

Rnds 22 and 23: Sc in each sc around.

Rnd 24: Sc in next 8 sc, 2 sc in next sc, (sc in next 16 sc, 2 sc in next sc) twice, sc in next 8 sc: 54 sc.

Rnd 25: Sc in each sc around.

Rnd 26: (Sc in next 17 sc, 2 sc in next sc) around: 57 sc.

Rnd 27: Sc in each sc around.

Rnd 28: Sc in next 9 sc, 2 sc in next sc, (sc in next 18 sc, 2 sc in next sc) twice, sc in next 9 sc: 60 sc.

Rnd 29: (2 Sc in next sc, sc in next 9 sc) around: 66 sc.

Rnds 30-37: Sc in each sc around.

Rnd 38: Slip st in each sc around; finish off.

CHOCOLATE DROP PILLOW

EASY

Finished Size: 16" (40.5 cm) diameter

shopping list

Yarn (Super Bulky Weight) SUPER BULKY 6
[6 ounces, 106 yards (170 grams, 97 meters) per skein]:
- ○ 2 skeins

Crochet Hook
- ○ Size M/N (9 mm) **or** size needed for gauge

Additional Supplies
- ○ 16" (40.5 cm) round pillow form

gauge information

Gauge Swatch: 4¼" (10.75 cm) diameter
Work same as Back on page 38 through Rnd 2: 18 dc and 6 Puff Sts.

stitch guide

PUFF STITCH (uses one dc)
★ YO, insert hook from **front** to **back** around post of dc just made ***(Fig. 3, page 43)***, YO and pull up a loop; repeat from ★ once **more**, YO and draw through all 5 loops on hook.

back

Ch 4; join with slip st to form a ring.

Rnd 1 (Right side)**:** Ch 3 **(counts as first dc, now and throughout)**, 11 dc in ring; join with slip st to first dc: 12 dc.

Note: Loop a short piece of yarn around any stitch to mark Rnd 1 as **right** side.

Rnd 2: Ch 3, dc in same st as joining, dc in next dc, work Puff St, ★ 2 dc in next dc, dc in next dc, work Puff St; repeat from ★ around; join with slip st to first dc: 18 dc and 6 Puff Sts.

Rnd 3: Ch 3, 2 dc in next dc, dc in next 2 dc, work Puff St, ★ dc in next dc, 2 dc in next dc, dc in next 2 dc, work Puff St; repeat from ★ around; join with slip st to first dc: 30 dc and 6 Puff Sts.

Rnd 4: Ch 3, dc in next dc, 2 dc in next dc, dc in next 3 dc, work Puff St, ★ dc in next 2 dc, 2 dc in next dc, dc in next 3 dc, work Puff St; repeat from ★ around; join with slip st to first dc: 42 dc and 6 Puff Sts.

Rnd 5: Ch 3, dc in next dc, 2 dc in next dc, dc in next 5 dc, work Puff St, ★ dc in next 2 dc, 2 dc in next dc, dc in next 5 dc, work Puff St; repeat from ★ around; join with slip st to first dc: 54 dc and 6 Puff Sts.

Rnd 6: Ch 3, dc in next 3 dc, 2 dc in next dc, dc in next 5 dc, work Puff St, ★ dc in next 4 dc, 2 dc in next dc, dc in next 5 dc, work Puff St; repeat from ★ around; join with slip st to first dc: 66 dc and 6 Puff Sts.

Rnd 7: Ch 3, dc in next 4 dc, 2 dc in next dc, dc in next 6 dc, work Puff St, ★ dc in next 5 dc, 2 dc in next dc, dc in next 6 dc, work Puff St; repeat from ★ around; join with slip st to first dc, finish off: 78 dc and 6 Puff Sts.

front

Work same as Back; at end of Rnd 7, do **not** finish off.

Ch 1; with **wrong** sides together, Front facing, and working through **both** sts on **both** pieces, sc in same st as joining and in each dc around, inserting pillow form before closing; join with slip st to first sc, finish off.

GENERAL INSTRUCTIONS

abbreviations

ch(s)......... chain(s)
cm............ centimeters
dc............. double crochet(s)
dc2tog..... double crochet 2 together
hdc........... half double crochet(s)
mm.......... millimeters
Rnd(s)...... Round(s)
sc............. single crochet(s)
sp(s)......... space(s)
st(s)......... stitch(es)
YO............ yarn over

symbols & terms

★ — work instructions following ★ as many **more** times as indicated in addition to the first time.

† to † — work all instructions from first † to second † **as many** times as specified.

( ) or [ ] — work enclosed instructions **as many** times as specified by the number immediately following **or** contains explanatory remarks.

colon (:) — the number(s) given after a colon at the end of a row or round denote(s) the number of stitches and spaces you should have on that row or round.

CROCHET TERMINOLOGY		
UNITED STATES		INTERNATIONAL
slip stitch (slip st)	=	single crochet (sc)
single crochet (sc)	=	double crochet (dc)
half double crochet (hdc)	=	half treble crochet (htr)
double crochet (dc)	=	treble crochet (tr)
treble crochet (tr)	=	double treble crochet (dtr)
double treble crochet (dtr)	=	triple treble crochet (ttr)
triple treble crochet (tr tr)	=	quadruple treble crochet (qtr)
skip	=	miss

CROCHET HOOKS																	
U.S.	B-1	C-2	D-3	E-4	F-5	G-6	7	H-8	I-9	J-10	K-10½	L-11	M/N-13	N/P-15	P/Q	Q	S
Metric - mm	2.25	2.75	3.25	3.5	3.75	4	4.5	5	5.5	6	6.5	8	9	10	15	16	19

Yarn Weight Symbol & Names	LACE 0	SUPER FINE 1	FINE 2	LIGHT 3	MEDIUM 4	BULKY 5	SUPER BULKY 6	JUMBO 7
Type of Yarns in Category	Fingering, size 10 crochet thread	Sock, Fingering, Baby	Sport, Baby	DK, Light Worsted	Worsted, Afghan, Aran	Chunky, Craft, Rug	Super Bulky, Roving	Jumbo, Roving
Crochet Gauge* Ranges in Single Crochet to 4" (10 cm)	32-42 sts**	21-32 sts	16-20 sts	12-17 sts	11-14 sts	8-11 sts	6-9 sts	5 sts and fewer
Advised Hook Size Range	Steel*** 6 to 8, Regular hook B-1	B-1 to E-4	E-4 to 7	7 to I-9	I-9 to K-10½	K-10½ to M/N-13	M/N-13 to Q	Q and larger

*GUIDELINES ONLY: The chart above reflects the most commonly used gauges and hook sizes for specific yarn categories.

** Lace weight yarns are usually crocheted with larger hooks to create lacy openwork patterns. Accordingly, a gauge range is difficult to determine. Always follow the gauge stated in your pattern.

*** Steel crochet hooks are sized differently from regular hooks–the higher the number, the smaller the hook, which is the reverse of regular hook sizing.

●○○○ **BEGINNER**	Projects for first-time crocheters using basic stitches. Minimal shaping.
●●○○ **EASY**	Projects using yarn with basic stitches, repetitive stitch patterns, simple color changes, and simple shaping and finishing.
●●●○ **INTERMEDIATE**	Projects using a variety of techniques, such as basic lace patterns or color patterns, mid-level shaping and finishing.
●●●● **EXPERIENCED**	Projects with intricate stitch patterns, techniques and dimension, such as non-repeating patterns, multi-color techniques, fine threads, small hooks, detailed shaping and refined finishing.

gauge

Exact gauge is essential for proper size. Before beginning your project, make the sample swatch given in the individual instructions in the yarn and hook specified. After completing the swatch, measure it, counting your stitches and rows or rounds carefully. If your swatch is larger or smaller than specified, **make another, changing hook size to get the correct gauge**. Keep trying until you find the size hook that will give you the specified gauge.

markers

Markers are used to help distinguish the beginning of each round being worked. Place a 2" (5 cm) scrap piece of yarn before the first stitch of each round, moving marker after each round is complete.

joining with sc

When instructed to join with sc, begin with a slip knot on hook. Insert hook in stitch or space indicated, YO and pull up a loop, YO and draw through both loops on hook.

joining with dc

When instructed to join with dc, begin with a slip knot on hook. YO, holding loop on hook, insert hook in stitch or space indicated, YO and pull up a loop (3 loops on hook), (YO and draw through 2 loops on hook) twice.

back ridge

Fig. 1

Work only in loops indicated by arrows *(Fig. 1)*.

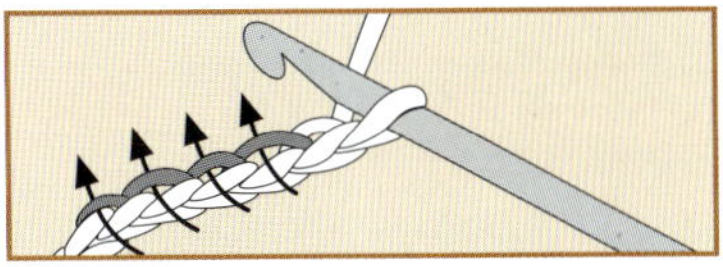

back loops only

Fig. 2

Work only in loop(s) indicated by arrows *(Fig. 2)*.

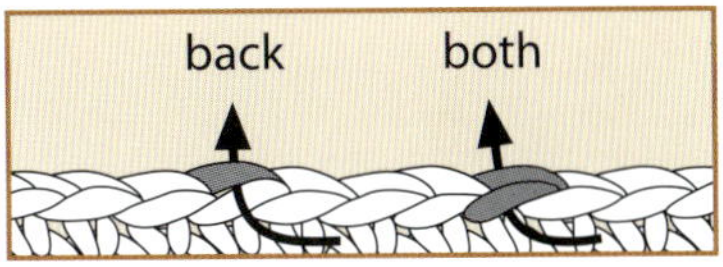

working around dc

Fig. 3

Insert hook from **front** to **back** around post of dc just made *(Fig. 3)*.

changing colors

Work last stitch to within one step of completion, hook new yarn ***(Fig. 4a or 4b)***, YO and draw through both loops on hook.

Fig. 4a

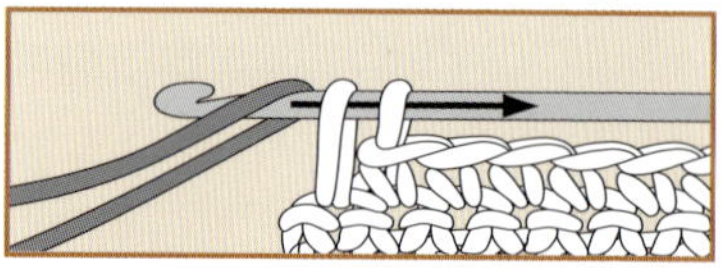

Fig. 4b

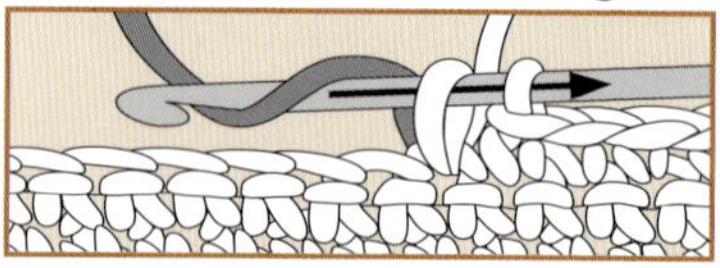

tassel

Cut a piece of cardboard 3" (7.5 cm) wide and as long as you want your finished tassel to be. Wind a double strand of yarn lengthwise around the cardboard approximately 16 times. Cut an 18" (45.5 cm) length of yarn and insert it under all of the strands at the top of the cardboard; pull up tightly and tie securely. Leave the yarn ends long enough to attach the tassel. Cut the yarn at the opposite end of the cardboard and then remove it ***(Fig. 5a)***. Cut a 6" (15 cm) length of yarn and wrap it tightly around the tassel twice, 1" (2.5 cm) below the top ***(Fig. 5b)***; tie securely. Trim the ends.

Fig. 5a

Fig. 5b

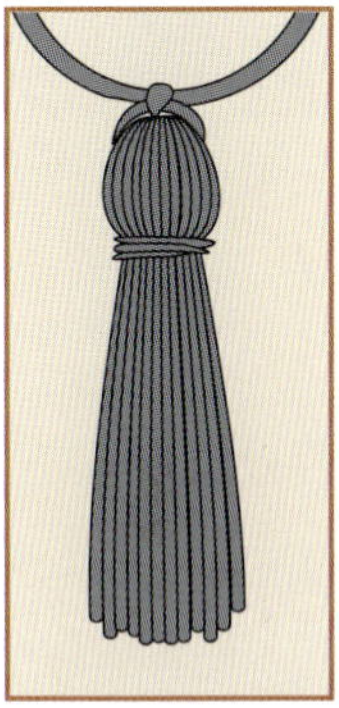

YARN INFORMATION

The items in this book were made using a variety of yarns. Any brand of the specific weight of yarn may be used. It is best to refer to the yardage/meters when determining how many balls or skeins to purchase. Remember, to achieve the same look, it is the weight of yarn that is important, not the brand of yarn.

For your convenience, listed on page 47 are the specific yarns used to create our photography models. Because yarn manufacturers make frequent changes to their product lines, you may sometimes find it necessary to use a substitute yarn or to search for the discontinued product at alternate suppliers (locally or online).

ALABASTER AFGHAN
Lion Brand® Wool-Ease® Thick & Quick®
#099 Fisherman

STILL FOG BASKET
Bernat® Maker Home Dec™
Taupe - #11008 Clay
Cream - #11009 Cream

FAWNBAY FLOOR PILLOW
Lion Brand® Wool-Ease® Thick & Quick®
Brown - #532 Toffee
Dk Brown - #404 Wood
Cream - #099 Fisherman

GO-GO GARLAND
Red Heart® Soft®
Green - #9522 Leaf
Dk Orange - #9263 Cinnabar
Purple - #9779 Berry
Teal - #9518 Teal
Lt Orange - #4422 Tangerine
Lt Gold - #9388 Wheat

THROW RUG
Lion Brand® Fast Track®
Taupe - #122 Truckers Taupe
Navy - #108 Dune Buggy Denim
Pink - #195 Pink Convertible

BLOSSOM FRAMES
Lion Brand® 24/7 Cotton®
Taupe - #122 Taupe
Blue - #108 Denim
Lt Blue - #107 Sky
Ecru - #098 Ecru

TOASTY TASSELS PILLOW
Lion Brand® Wool-Ease® Thick & Quick®
#536 Fossil

FLOWERPOT COZIES
Bernat® Pop!™
#84005 Planetary

CHOCOLATE DROP PILLOW
Lion Brand® Wool-Ease® Thick & Quick®
#122 Taupe

MEET EDIE ECKMAN

Years ago Edie Eckman co-owned a yarn shop. The work severely limited her time to knit and crochet, so she closed the shop after a while and turned to designing.

"Now I have my fingers in many aspects of the fiber arts," Edie says. She teaches her popular workshops at Stitches, the National Needlearts Association, Crochet Guild of America and The Knitting Guild of America conferences and other national venues, as well as at local shops and guilds. "I love the 'a-ha' moment when a student gains a new bit of understanding," she says.

When Edie wants to unplug from her fast-paced work life, she heads for the woods. "We have a little cabin. There's no TV or Internet service. I love to go there for walks and to paddle around the lake. However, I've always got designs in my head, ready to be sold."

To see Edie's workshop schedule, visit her Web site at EdieEckman.com. She can also be found on Facebook as EdieEckman, as well as on Ravelry. Look for other Leisure Arts books featuring Edie's designs at www.leisurearts.com/meet-the-designers/edie-eckman.html.

Production Team: Instructional/Technical Editor - Sarah J. Green; Senior Graphic Artist - Lora Puls; Graphic Artists - Shell Stoll and Amy L. Teeter; Photo Stylist - Lori Wenger; and Photographer - Jason Masters.

Made in China